...pire you
to create your own more
personal prayers too.

When you enter a house, first say, 'Peace to this house.' Luke 10:5

I will pray
with my spirit,
but I will pray
with my mind also;
I will sing
praise with my
spirit, but I will sing
with my mind also.
Cor. 14:15

Praying through your
home and neighbourhood will
make a difference. When we
invite God into our everyday
living space we invite God to
participate in the little things
of our life, the humdrum and
the ordinary, and even the
boring. Those things probably
won't suddenly be
transformed into amazing
spiritual experiences but
there will be a difference.

x Mary

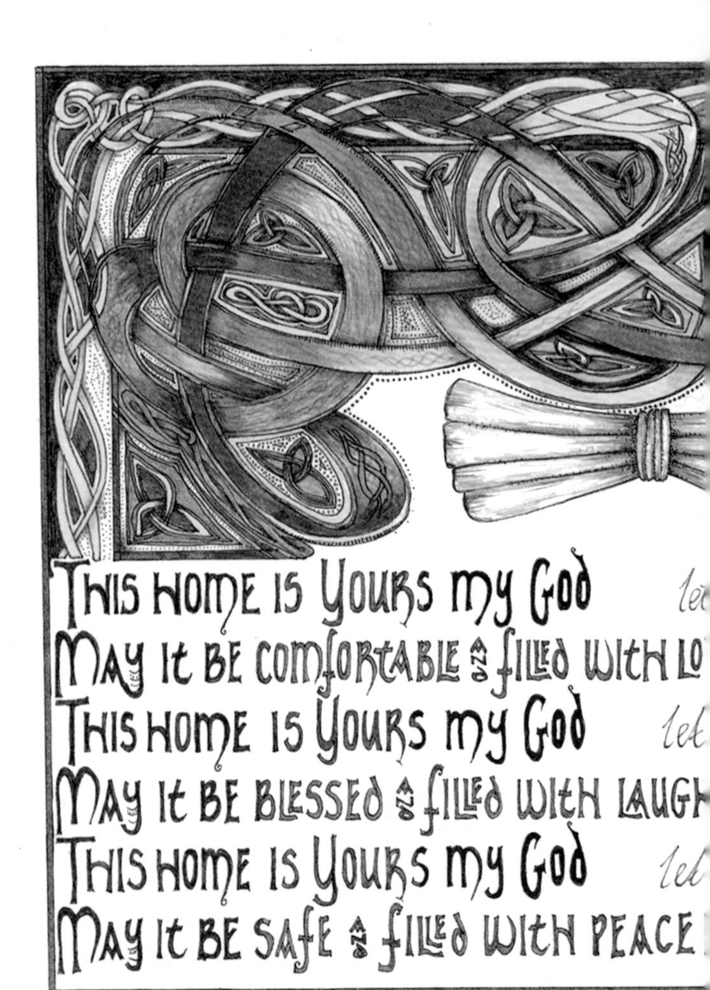
THIS HOME IS YOURS MY GOD
MAY IT BE COMFORTABLE AND FILLED WITH
THIS HOME IS YOURS MY GOD let
MAY IT BE BLESSED AND FILLED WITH
THIS HOME IS YOURS MY GOD let
MAY IT BE SAFE AND FILLED WITH PEACE

be
LIGHT
be
JOY
be
OPE

The piece 'Home Blessing' shown on the pages before features the cross of St. Brigid. The legend tells that she wove the cross at the death bed of either her father or a pagan lord, who upon hearing what the cross meant, asked to be baptized. One version goes as follows:

> 'A pagan chieftain from the neighbourhood of Kildare was dying. Christians in his household sent for Brigid to talk to him about Christ. When she arrived, the chieftain was raving. As it was impossible to instruct this delirious man, hopes for his conversion seemed doubtful. Brigid sat down at his bedside and began consoling him. As was customary, the dirt floor was strewn with rushes both for warmth and cleanliness. Brigid stooped down and started to weave them into a cross, fastening the points together. The sick man asked what she was doing. She began to explain the cross, and as she talked, his delirium quieted and he questioned her with growing interest. Through her weaving, he converted and was baptized at the point of death. Since then, the cross of rushes has existed in Ireland.' ©Wikipedia

There may be an earlier, pagan, origin of the cross but, like many legends the story has blurred over time

Front door

Bless all who enter through this door,
Whether family, stranger or friend,
If any don't yet know You,
Let them find You inside.

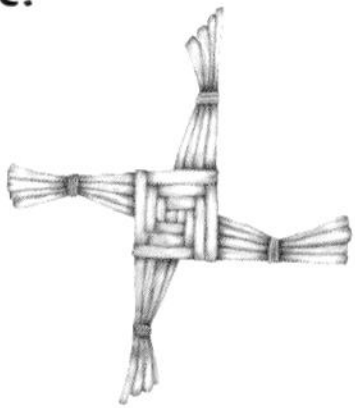

Bless all who enter through this door,
Whether they care for me or not,
If You will give me the grace,
Let them find love inside.

Bless all who leave through this door,
May they carry Your peace as they go.
Protect them as they depart,
Protect me when I leave.
And protect my home,
Until I return.

Hallway

As I breathe a sigh and close the door,
May this hallway feel safe and welcoming.

Help me to give my burdens to You...

As I prepare to leave and open the door,
May I sense Your presence walking beside me.

Help me to see You in the stranger's face...

Living Room

In my rest I praise You,
In my activity I praise You,
In my joys I praise You,
In my sadness I praise You,
In my peace I praise You,
In my conflict I praise You.

As this room is witness
to all my ways of being
May I welcome Your involvement,
And above all may this room
be a safe place
To simply be.

Kitchen/Dining Room

Bless the preparing and the cooking,
Bless the eating and the drinking,
Bless the times alone and the times with others.

A room used for work

Bless the work of my hands,
May they be sure and strong,
Bless the workings of my mind,
May my thinking be clear and quick,
Bless my concentration,
May it be unwavering,
Bless my breaks,
May I remember to take them.

Bedroom

May no unpleasant thoughts or dreams disturb.
May resting minds be filled with peace.
May aches and pains diminish.
May troubles stay outside the door.
May sleep restore and strengthen.

A Child's Bedroom

Fill this room with Your presence,
Protect and keep n. safe,
May night-time dreams
be filled with good things,
May day-time dreams
have no limits,
May illness be rare
and health be embraced,
Protect and keep n. safe,
Fill this room and her/his/their life/lives
with Your presence.

n. = name

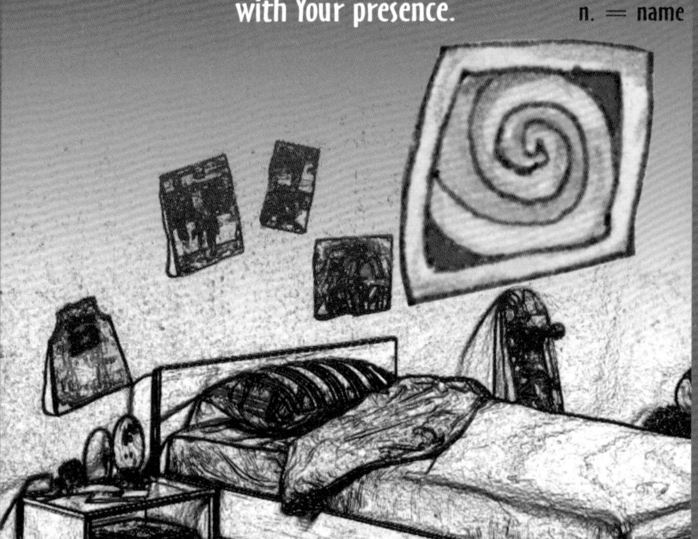

A teenager's bedroom

Fill this room with Your presence,
Protect and keep n. safe.

In the midst of confusion
may this room bring peace,
Protect and keep n. safe.

In the midst of angst
may this room bring sanctuary,
Protect and keep n. safe.

In the midst of heartache
may this room bring comfort,
Protect and keep n. safe.

In the midst of awareness
may this room bring simplicity.
Protect and keep n. safe.

Fill this room and her/his life
with Your presence.

Garden/Yard

I call protection on this land,
May it be fruitful in every way needed.

May it provide the joy of inspiration,
The satisfaction of tenderness,
The reward of labour,
The challenge of time,

And the peace of the open sky.

At each door and window -

(and on walls, ceilings and floors)

I make the sign of the cross.
Let nothing that is not of You enter here,
Let everything that is not of You leave.

In each room -

Fill this space with Your presence,
Fill each dark corner with Your light.
In the name of our Creator God,
our Saviour Jesus
and our Holy Companion, The Spirit.
Amen.

Around the outside of a property -

(local prayer walk)

Loving God, please see the people
who live in this place,
Hear their cries, those that are silent too.
May they desire to know You,
or know You more,
May they have opportunity to meet You, often.
Help me to be a loving neighbour and a friend.
Please bless and protect the people
who live in this place.

How to make a Brigid Cross...

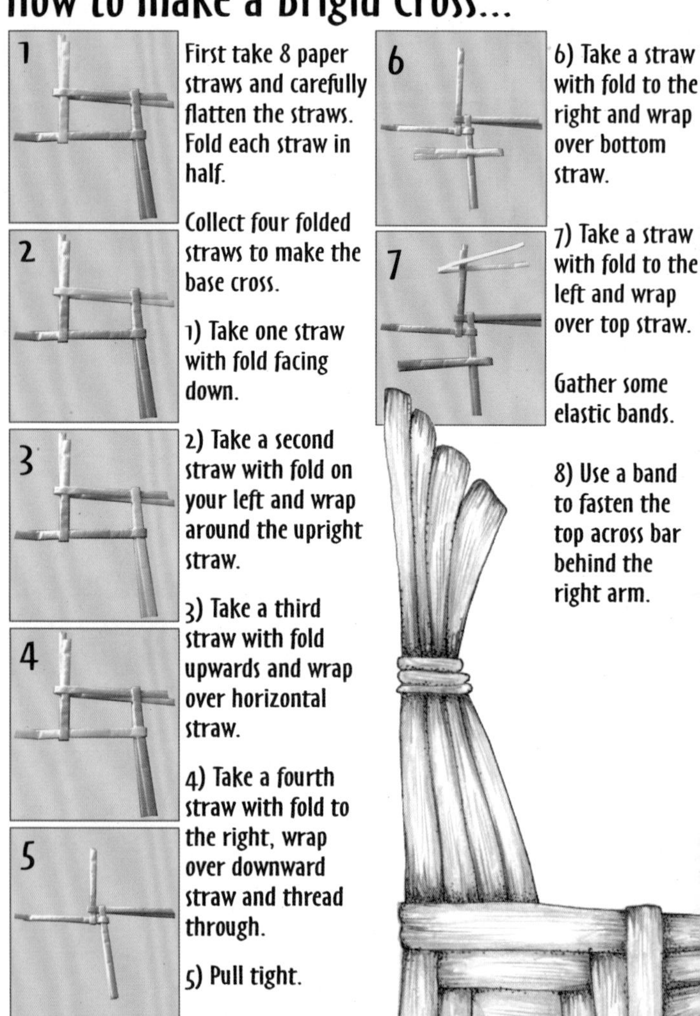

First take 8 paper straws and carefully flatten the straws. Fold each straw in half.

Collect four folded straws to make the base cross.

1) Take one straw with fold facing down.

2) Take a second straw with fold on your left and wrap around the upright straw.

3) Take a third straw with fold upwards and wrap over horizontal straw.

4) Take a fourth straw with fold to the right, wrap over downward straw and thread through.

5) Pull tight.

6) Take a straw with fold to the right and wrap over bottom straw.

7) Take a straw with fold to the left and wrap over top straw.

Gather some elastic bands.

8) Use a band to fasten the top across bar behind the right arm.

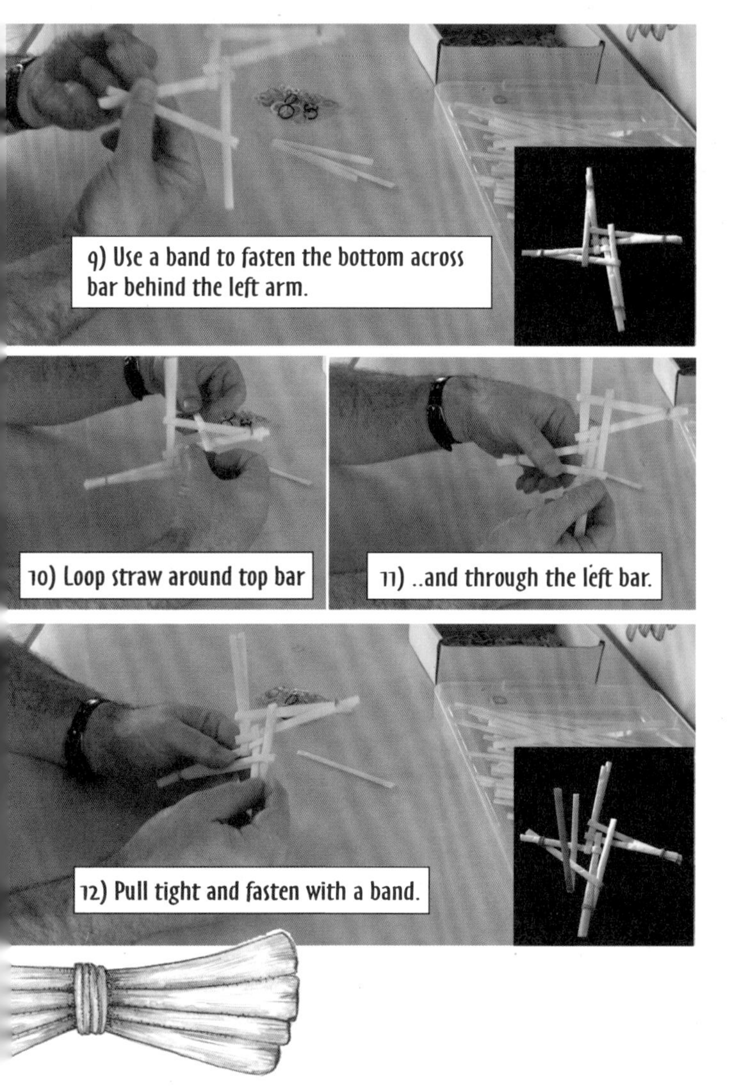
9) Use a band to fasten the bottom across bar behind the left arm.
10) Loop straw around top bar
11) ..and through the left bar.
12) Pull tight and fasten with a band.

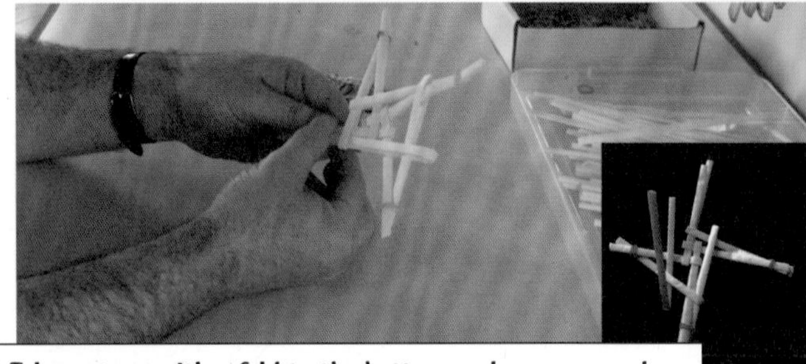

13) Take a straw with a fold to the bottom and wrap around bottom bar and then over the left arm and through the rightward arm.

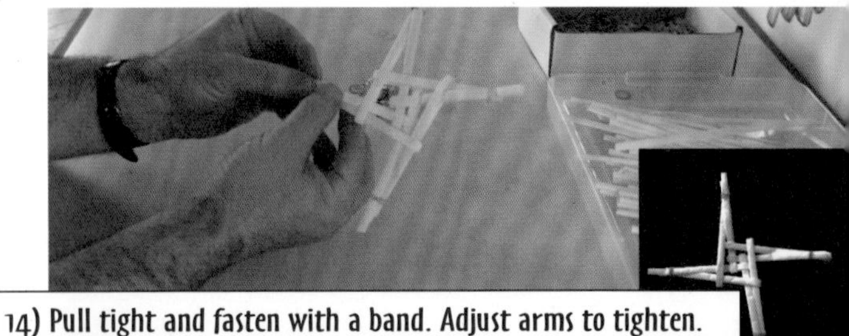

14) Pull tight and fasten with a band. Adjust arms to tighten.

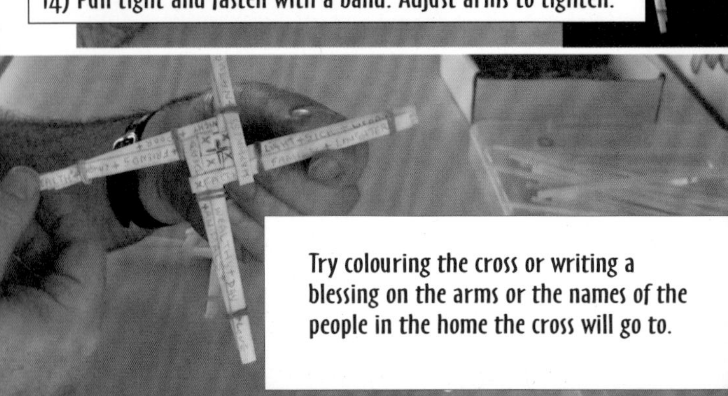

Try colouring the cross or writing a blessing on the arms or the names of the people in the home the cross will go to.

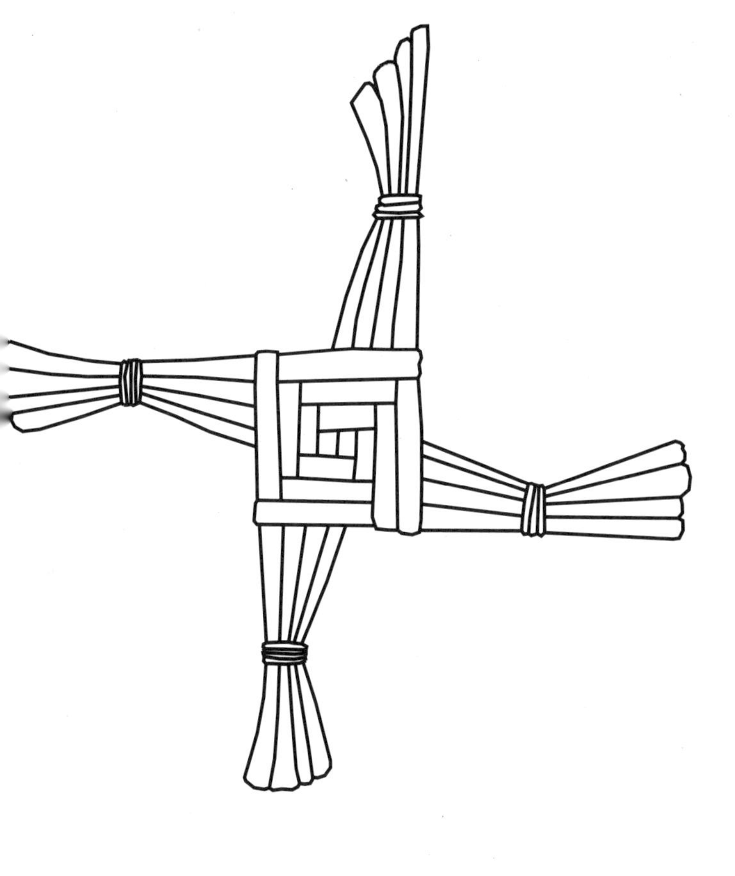

Colour and cut out the Brigid Cross above and stick it on a wall or door - there's also the reverse printed on the other side so that you could colour both sides and hang the cross from a ceiling. You may also photocopy the Brigid cross image (but please not anything else from the book).